CW00731239

HAPPY CHILDREN

A Step-by-Step Parenting Guide: How to
Raise Girls and Boys without Ranting,
Encourage their Talents, and Deal with their
Strengths and Weaknesses the Right Way

Pia W. Davies

Copyright © [2021] [Pia W. Davies]

All rights reserved.

The author of this book owns the exclusive right to its content.

Any commercial usage or reproduction requires the clear consent of the author.

ISBN – 9798720930837

Table of Contents

Introduction

It's challenging to be a parent – there's no doubt about that. The fact that you have found your way to this book only confirms that you want to be the best possible parent you can be. Unfortunately, life gets busy, and it's easy to get that "not now, maybe later" approach to parenting. This book is aimed at parents just like you. This book is for parents who feel like they have dropped the ball or need a helping hand to get their parenting back on track, to ensure a bright and happy future for their children. By reading this book, you are equipping yourself for champion parenting, which is nearly as much a journey of self-discovery for you as it is about raising content, happy, and grounded children.

One certain thing is that children need structure and discipline. They need parents who are present in all senses of the word. More importantly, they need parents who are willing to guide them and put in the effort to ensure that they become well-rounded, confident, happy, and deeply fulfilled adults.

You may look at other parents who seem to have a knack for raising highly-successful, contributing members of society and wonder how they do it without ranting, stressing-out, and failing consistently. The truth of the matter is that to be the type of parent that raises happy boys and girls in a patient and wholesome way is not rocket science. It's merely about having a parenting strategy and committing to work at it every single day. Once you know what to do to help your children become the best they can be, it becomes a little easier.

The process of raising happy children is not all sunshine and rainbows, mind you. You're going to have good days and bad days, and so are your children. The best thing you can do is to approach the process with unconditional love and a commitment to be there to support and guide your children no matter what. *That* type of parent is the best possible parent a child could ever hope for.

What Makes Children Happy?

It's not toys, expensive clothes, and exhilarating holidays that make children deeply happy. Yes, these material things are fun and exciting for children, and they do provide a certain amount of happiness, but this type of happiness is not long-term and doesn't practically prepare children for real life. That said, before we leap into the very first chapter of this book; let's consider 12 signs that children are truly happy.

Happy children with a balanced and bright future:

- Make good choices.

- Know right from wrong.

- Feel heard and understood.

- Are responsible and reliable.

- Have a positive attitude/outlook.

- Know how to enjoy good clean fun.

- They are confident and have good self-esteem.

- Have access to a healthy, nourishing lifestyle.

- Can recognise a healthy and happy relationship.

- Receive (and know how to give) unconditional love.

- Know how to express their emotions and communicate openly.

- Know how to connect with and form relationships with others.

To ensure your children make progress in the right areas of their lives (and development), prepare to put in the work. So let's jump right in and get started.

Overview

There is no "one thing" that you can do to ensure that your children grow up happy, content, and well-rounded. Instead, it is a combination of things that you need to do over an extended time. This book aims to address 12 ways you can raise happier and more confident children.

Each chapter applies to children of all ages and will help any parent of any background. The 12 chapters featured cover the following topics and categories.

1. Prioritising self-care

2. Creating an element of positive thinking

3. Implementing family responsibilities

4. Praising correctly

5. Approaching discipline calmly

6. Creating family rituals

7. Creating and exploring interests

8. Teaching children to manage emotions

9. Helping children build meaningful relationships

10. The importance of implementing (and teaching) a healthy daily schedule

11. Teaching action and consequence

12. Importance of prioritising your marriage / relationship

If you are ready to take your parenting skills to the next level and see your children grow and prosper from strength to strength, delve into the chapters to follow.

Chapter One: Prioritising Self-Care

Many parents aren't aware of this, but practising self-care is an essential part of being a good parent and raising happy children.

Parents, as leaders of the family, have to be at their very best to lead effectively. If your morale is low, you're looking shabby, and you're tired and worn out, you're not going to be able to carry out your parenting duties to your full potential. What's worse is that you will be setting the bar for your children. They may grow up to believe that they can let themselves go and that it's normal to be tired, overworked, worn out, stressed, and dishevelled. They may even get the idea that they don't deserve or need self-care because they never really saw it in action at home.

Developing a good self-image is about practising self-care, and the only way you can encourage your children to practice self-care is to set a good example. If you don't take good care of yourself, you can't teach your children to care for themselves.

Ditch the Guilt and Create a Self-Care Schedule

Before we take a look at how you can incorporate self-care into your life in a way that gets your children's attention, let's get something straight; self-care is not selfish! It's one of the most important things you can teach your children. So don't feel guilty when you schedule time away from the family to recoup, revive, and replenish yourself. Soon, you will feel motivated and even inspired to get right back to whipping up sumptuous nourishing meals and collecting stuffed-animal toys from every conceivable surface and your children will notice.

Below are a few ways that you can incorporate self-care into your life:

- Schedule a soak in the tub one night a week.

- Go to a movie with a friend.

- Commit to grooming (shaving, colouring your hair, cutting your nails).

- Head out for a weekend gym session followed by a coffee on the way home.

- Hire a babysitter and schedule a date night with your partner (twice a month should be manageable).

- Schedule time to enjoy your hobbies at home.

Allow your children to see you practising self-care and encourage them to do the same.

Children Need Me-Time Too

Many parents wrongly believe that academics and sports are the main focuses of a child's life, but that's just not true. Self-care is just as important.

Children who are taught about self-care, and practice it from a young age, learn to identify their physical and emotional needs, and are better equipped to deal with them.

There are various ways to teach children the importance of self-care, and it's not all about bubble baths and nail-painting. Instead, it's about teaching children how to tend to their own needs without always coming to you to do things *for* them. As part of self-care, children need to learn to be independent (do things for themselves), know how to have fun, care for their bodies, and self-soothe. Here's how you can help your children in these areas.

Teaching children to be independent

How often do you find yourself in a hurry (most parents are, don't worry), so you end up doing things *for* your children that they should probably do for themselves? You could be delaying your child from developing healthy independence. Of course, you don't need to leave your children stranded with no help, but when they ask you for something, consider if it is a task they can handle themselves.

Some tasks that can help a child learn independence include: tying shoelaces, picking up toys after a day of playing, pouring a glass of water, making a snack (or helping with preparation), carrying school bags, washing dishes, picking out clothes for the day, getting dressed, and putting dirty clothes in the laundry basket. These are just examples. If you think of more tasks your children can cope with, add them to your list and make yourself a little less available to assist with them. Do this with kindness, of course. Try to encourage your children to carry out tasks they haven't done before and praise them when they try. A great way to get a smaller child on board with this is to use the correct language. You can say something like, "Which of these tasks do you feel you are big enough to help with?" Children who learn to be independent at a young age grow up feeling empowered.

Teaching children how to create fun for themselves

Society has done a great job of teaching children that fun exists on a television screen. If you have the type of children that spend a large part of their free time glued to the television or device screen, you need to re-teach them the meaning of fun. Well-rounded children have healthy stress levels, which requires more than just a few hours of their favourite cartoon.

Children need to be active, get silly, be creative, blow off steam, and get those good-feeling endorphins flowing. To get your children interested, be prepared to get involved and have some fun yourself.

Fun activities to incorporate into daily life include pillow fights, baking, bubble blowing and impromptu dance parties. Other fun options include:

- Hide-and-seek.

- Art (drawing or painting).

- Bike riding.

- Going for a walk.

- Playing with the pets.

- Playing board games.

- Reading a fun book (story-time as a family is a great idea).

Teaching children how to care for their bodies (and physical needs)

Physical health is vitally important to your child's happiness. As a parent, it is your job to set a good example and encourage your child to incorporate healthy physical self-care practices into his/her life. Areas you should focus on include:

- Exercise

  One of the first things that you should focus on is encouraging your children to do some form of exercise. If you go to the gym, consider taking your children with you. Of course, if your children are very young, this may not be an option. You can also encourage exercise by playing games like soccer, catches, and running races. Going on regular family walks is also a good option. Make sure that you explain the importance of exercise to your children. It's good for physical fitness, heart health and spurs on good mental health too.

- Personal hygiene

    Happy, well-rounded children know how to take care of their hygiene needs. You should spend some time teaching your children how to do the following on their own: bath/shower, brush and style hair, brush and floss teeth, trim nails, wash hands, blow noses, and change dirty clothing when required.

- Teaching children how to self-soothe (manage emotions)

    Children who don't know how to self-soothe may become overwhelmed with emotions because they have no outlet. Teaching your children to deal with their feelings healthily is vitally important to their long-term happiness. Emotions that children often struggle to make sense of and control include anger, frustration, jealousy, sadness, and fear. You can equip your children with the tools required to deal with these emotions by talking to them about each feeling. Explain the emotions and why they may be feeling that way. Also, provide your children with a list (this can grow over time) of healthy things they can do to deal with each of these emotions. Various activities can help children healthily work through their emotions. Consider the following:

- Talk to your children about their feelings and urge them to tell you how they feel as often as possible. Just talking about it and feeling heard can be a great release.

- Breathing and counting exercises can help a child to simmer down before reacting to feelings of anger and jealousy. Teach your children a few basic exercises (there are loads to choose from online).

- Listening to music is something that can help children of all ages to keep calm and feel happier. Expose your children to various genres and make a playlist of their favourites.

- High-energy sports/activities such as running, punching (you may need to get a punching bag), or going for a bike ride can help children gather their thoughts and calm down.

- Writing about it (for children who are old enough) can be an excellent outlet for all emotions, ranging from happiness to outrage. Gift your child with a journal and encourage him/her to spend time writing about their day and feelings before going to bed each night. Make sure that your children know that their journals are for their eyes only.

- Consistently talk about *all* feelings and emotions, even the good and positive ones. When someone is happy, discuss this with your children and ask them to share it with you when they are happy too. It will help them to become more comfortable with talking about feelings and emotions in the future.

Chapter Two: Creating an Element of Positive Thinking

It's important to teach your children to look on the bright side of life from an early age. Pre-teens who already have a positive outlook on life will be less prone to grouchy teenage behaviour. That should be enough to motivate you!

Raising optimists isn't particularly hard, but it all starts with you. Are you a positive thinker? Do you have an optimistic outlook? If you don't, the work needs to begin with you. Change how you react to the world around you. Remember that children will notice what you say *and* how you react, so you can't say something positive and pair it with a sullen look or body language that belies what you say. Be the type of person who embraces good things and celebrates the small wins in life. Embracing the small wins will be of high-value to your child's overall happiness.

We could all do with a little positivity, so put some time and effort into celebrating the good things in life and giving less air time to the bad things that may happen. In general, positive thinkers and optimists are:

- More successful at school, work, and sports.

- Less prone to mental health issues.

- More satisfied in their relationships.

- Less likely to suffer depression and anxiety.

- Generally healthier.

- Less prone to stress-related illness, such as cardiovascular disease and high blood pressure.

- Stronger in terms of immunity.

These are just a few of the benefits of being a positive thinker. Don't you want to ensure these benefits for your children? Of course, you do!

5 Ways to Teach Children to be Naturally More Positive

Let's take a look at a few activities (and things you can do) to help your children foster a positive attitude towards life.

Make positive notes

End each day on a positive note with your child. After the regular bedtime routine, ask your child to help you come up with a positive thought for the next day. It can be silly or significant. You can use a Google or Pinterest search for inspiration by merely searching "positive life quotes" or "positive quotes for kids". Write the chosen quote down on a post-it note and stick it onto the bathroom mirror for the next morning. Keep all the notes in a notebook or journal to be reviewed at the end of the year.

Create a 'life's good' journal with your children

Creating a journal is a project for the whole family. Buy a notebook or journal and keep it in a family area (the kitchen or living room are great spots). Each week, each family member should create a page that features something small that makes life good in a simple way. It could be the fact that you baked biscuits earlier that week, and your child loved the smell of freshly baked biscuits wafting through the house. It could be the sheer joy of an overflowing bubble bath. Each page should be colourful, happy, and share a positive thought. Everyone should be allowed to admire each other's pages with a suitable amount of oohing and aahing.

Share fun and positive stories with your children

If something funny and positive happened during the day, tell your children about it. Be animated about it and make sure to communicate how happy and uplifted the experience made you feel. Laugh about these experiences and encourage your children to share some funny stories of their own. When your children share a positive or fun story with you, take the time to engage and listen to what they are saying. Try to see the fun or positive side and laugh along. Turn your home into the type of place where positive stories are praised and enjoyed and where gossip, down talk, and negative tales, are given far less attention. Creating a positive space will set the tone for the type of information and stories your children see worthy of sharing. It will equip them to become adults who don't involve themselves in petty chit-chat or unkind rumours.

Encourage your children to carry out acts of service

Well-rounded and happy children are those who realise how fortunate they are. They are children who are willing to go the extra mile for someone else. If you want children who aren't selfish or self-centred, encourage them to practice acts of service. When children start to realise how much of a difference they can make, it can empower them and develop a deeply rooted sense of self-confidence and self-worth. What your child can do:

- Yard work for an elderly neighbour.

- Plan a surprise for another family member.

- Volunteer at an animal shelter or soup kitchen.

- Gather a bag of small toys to donate to a charity shop or children's home. You can set an excellent example by adding a few of your own goodies to the pile.

- Write regular letters to aunts, uncles, and grandparents.

- Bake a cake or biscuits for the neighbours.

- Help a sibling with a chore.

- Let a stranger cut in front of you in line (you may have to encourage this by setting an example).

- Create home recycling projects.

These are just a few basic ideas. Gather the family together to create a list of possible acts of service *with* your children. You may be pleasantly surprised at how kind they want to be.

Expose your children to fun and positive books

Reading is an essential part of a child's development. Happy children have imagination, and while movies can provide entertainment, they aren't nearly as nourishing for the imagination as books are. You can use books to get your children thinking positively and seeing the bright side of life. As they grow older, this thinking will filter into how they view the world and life in general. There are many great children's book authors out there, with a few of the classics including Enid Blyton (particularly *The Faraway Tree* and *The Wishing Chair*), Roald Dahl, David Williams, B.J Novak (particularly *The Book with No Pictures*).

What to Do if You Have Negative Children

Are your children already on a negative path? You may think that it's too late, but it's not! It's never too late to start working on behavioural changes. Here's how you can help children prone to negative thinking, whinging, whining, and complaining.

Stop complaining (yes, you!)

Children are like sponges. They watch and absorb everything their parents do. If you act and react negatively to the world around you, your children will assume that it's the norm. Stop and adopt a positive outlook and approach.

Start building an attitude of gratitude

Get the whole family to participate in a gratitude exercise briefly every evening mealtime. Each person at the table should share one thing that they are grateful or thankful for that day. If your children find it hard to think of something they are thankful for, they can share a positive thought or a joke that the family might enjoy. Make this a compulsory exercise and get everyone involved. Treat it as a type of family "homework".

Encourage your child to think about things from a different angle

Children can get stuck in a negative thought pattern, especially when things don't go their way. Try to help them see that something negative doesn't always have to be focused on. Negatives can be turned into positives. For instance, if your child comes second in class or a race, you can teach them that yes, maybe they aren't the best in the class or the fastest in a race, but there are other areas of their lives where they excel, and others don't. Remind your children of how they shine.

Encourage a problem-solving approach

Children who think negatively often see a problem in everything. They also believe that they can't do things. Have you ever heard your child whining, "I can't!" when asked to try something new? That's a problem! If your child faces a problem, ask him/her to write it down. Then, work together, brainstorming possible solutions to the problem or negative thought. Try to encourage your child to participate and then build and expand on the ideas that he/she provides. At the end of the exercise, decide together which of the suggested solutions aren't feasible. Then, ask your child to select one of the viable options and try it out. It will take some time for this exercise to start working, but be consistent and work with your child regularly on this type of positive problem-solving task. A change of mindset doesn't happen overnight, but it certainly *can* happen.

Chapter Three: Implementing Family Responsibilities

Many parents worry about giving their children chores, and that's normal. After all, you probably feel as if running the household is your responsibility. And it is. Children need to feel as if they are part of the "community" and can't feel that way if they have everything done for them, and nothing is expected from them. To be a respected and needed member of *any* community, a person (regardless of age) needs to feel needed, important and necessary. Chores can achieve a sense of belonging. When you expect something of your children, it drives the message home that you care about them and that they are part of the team; they are *needed.* Children that feel this way are generally happy.

Of course, you don't need to give your children a to-do list as long as your arm or with difficult chores attached, but you can give them a few things to do around the house that benefit the entire family.

Studies have shown that children who have chores from an early age are more likely to be happy and independent adults. In fact, in a Harvard Study held over 75 years, researchers found that children who had chores are more likely to have part-time jobs or participate in sports and school clubs as they get older. That said, you may be depriving your children of a good work ethic by *not* giving them chores.

The trick with chores is to start with them as early as possible so that your child sees it as a fun activity and not a task. However, if you have missed the boat and your children are already primary schoolers, tweens or teens, it's not too late. You have to approach the subject gently and prescribe age-appropriate chores.

If your children throw tantrums, don't back down and scrap the chores idea. Be persistent and gentle but firm. Creating chores for the home is one of the first steps for ensuring children grow up happy, well-balanced, and responsible.

Chores to Give Your Children

Let's take a look at what chores you can assign to children at various ages/stages.

Pre-schoolers

Try to keep it simple with pre-school children. They may need a little help at this age, and you may need to make it fun, like a game. Creating a sticker chart to award gold stars with every completed chore is a great way to inspire co-operation. Here are some chores you can ask your pre-schooler to help you with:

- Pick up toys lying in the house and pack them away.

- Put dirty clothes in the washing basket at the end of each day.

- Pack some of the dishes away during clean up.

Primary School Children

When your children progress from pre-school to "big school", it's time to increase their chores too. They should still clean up after themselves, but you can add a few extra tasks to the list. Here are some to consider:

- Pack away backpacks and shoes after school

- Wash the dishes after mealtime

- Help with food preparation

- Set the table for meals

- Take out the trash on certain days of the week

Remember to thank your children after they have completed their chores. They will feel appreciated.

Tweens (Pre-teens)

It's usually at pre-teens age where children start wanting an allowance (aka "pocket money"). You can use this stage to reward your child for certain chores financially and then teach them a bit about financial responsibility. Some great tasks for pre-teens include:

- Cleaning the bathroom

- Sweeping, mopping, vacuuming

- Making up their bed

- Walking the dog (if you have one)

- Simple garden chores

- Packing their clean laundry away

There is a great variety of mobile apps, for example GoHenry, that you can use to set your children custom tasks. When children complete the tasks, a portion of their pocket money goes into their account. Children can spend their money at pre-determined stores, and as a parent, you have access to seeing how they spend their money. These apps teach young children about financial responsibility. As far as raising happy children goes, such apps are a great tool to help in the process, and really can help you get your tweens on board with chores.

Teenagers

Teenagers can be a little trickier to get on board with chores, but they need to contribute to the family unit. Below are a few tasks that are appropriate for teens:

- Doing their laundry (or doing the family's laundry)

- Helping with folding and packing away laundry

- Cooking a meal once a week

- Washing and packing away dishes

- Helping with grocery shopping (and packing away)

- Handling the household recycling

- Occasionally helping younger siblings with their homework and chores

- Babysitting younger siblings when required

You can continue to use the GoHenry app or pay your teenage children for their efforts.

How to introduce chores and responsibilities

If you're introducing chores and responsibilities to children who have never had to do them before, you might find yourself faced with some confusion and resistance. Remember not to lose your cool. Remain calm, loving, and kind. It's always best to explain why chores are necessary and drive home the underlying message that as a family (team), everyone must pull together to make it a pleasant and balanced experience for each other.

Below are a few things to keep in mind when introducing chores to your children:

- Set your expectations clearly and make sure your children understand what the actual chore is. Be clear by saying something like, "after dinner, you and your sister are going to wash and pack away the dishes."

- Get stuck in and help. If children feel as if the chores are for them alone, they may develop a negative approach. Instead, grab a kitchen towel and dry a few dishes or wipe counters while they work. Be around and be involved.

- Praise. Don't underestimate the power of positive feedback. Use recognition like "good job" or "great work" and even throw in a high-five or two.

- If your children refuse to do their chores or say they don't want to, don't shout or get into a rage. Instead, empathise with your child. Tell your children that you understand playing would be more fun, but there will be a negative outcome if they don't help with the chores. For example, you could say, "I know you don't want to help with the laundry and would rather text your friend, but then you won't have any clean clothes for the weekend". Be persuasive while still empathising.

Doing chores is part of a happy child's life, so spend some time reiterating that chores are a family responsibility and a sign of love for each other. Develop a motto of "When we all pull our weight, we all live comfortably."

Chapter Four: Praising Correctly

Parents across the world struggle to strike a balance when it comes to praising their children. They typically praise their children when they do something that requires effort, such as building a sandcastle, painting a beautiful picture, or winning a football match, and everything else too.

In the past, traditional parenting avoided praise because people thought it would cause their children to develop over-inflated egos. Much has changed, and scientific studies prove that praising, when done correctly, can be an excellent thing for children's overall happiness. However, mums and dads should be careful not to go the opposite way and over-praise.

Before we delve into why let's take a look at a few of the benefits of praising your children correctly:

- Praise keeps children engaging in projects, tasks, and activities.

- Giving praise nurtures a child's confidence and self-esteem.

- Praising teaches children to be proud of their achievements.

- Praise helps children try new things (and try harder at old things too).

- Praise leaves children feeling happy and noticed.

Now that you know that praise is significant, you're probably wondering a few more things, like how much credit you should give, when you should provide it, what the quality of praise should be, and so on. To give you some insight, let's move on to discussing how to use recognition correctly. When you get it right, you help your children build on themselves and become happier and more confident.

Using Praise The Right Way

Just like everything in life, there is a right and wrong way to praise your children. You're probably wondering how on earth that can be possible. Surely praise is praise, right? Wrong!

First and foremost, you have to use praise with caution. Some children respond well to praise, whereas other children feel uncomfortable and experience adverse effects. In addition to this, you can't dish out praise for every little thing that a child does because your praise will lose its value. Below are a few ways that you can praise your children constructively.

Be specific about what you are praising

Mention specific things that made you proud and be descriptive. It will help your children to see your praise as genuine and honest. And it will give them something to focus on when trying new things.

Always praise when your children try something new

You want your children to adopt an attitude of trying new things, so when they do, praise them and make them feel good about it.

Avoid praising too often or for *everything*

When you overdo it, the meaning behind the praise is lost, and soon the words become empty. The idea is to make your child excited by recognition and find depth in it. By praising too consistently, it won't have the desired effect.

Only praise genuinely and honestly

You may think that your children don't know when you are praising insincerely, but they do. Providing genuine praise is essential so that your children can trust your positive words (and rely on them).

Praise the effort put in and not the achievement/award

When you praise children for their efforts, they start to associate their efforts and hard work with the desired outcome: achievement and award. When you praise the achievement/award, children stop seeing their effort as the driving factor.

Avoid using conditional praise

Conditional praise sounds like this: "Great job! You did well, but I know you can do even better next time." This type of recognition can be encouraging to a child, but not always. Still, it may cause them to avoid certain activities in the future because the basis of future praise rests on whether or not they can do better (as is seemingly expected).

Avoid using comparison praise

Comparison praise is when you praise a child in such a way that they feel compared to someone else. For instance, you might say, "you are so good at running races, just like your brother." This praise is a dangerous type because when your children are winning, they will feel great about the comparison, but they will continue to compare and end up feeling bad about themselves when they lose.

How to Handle Negative Response to Praise

You might think that all children *should* love praise, and most of them do, but it doesn't always work out that way. Some children don't respond to praise as positively as most kids do. Instead, they wish the earth would open up and swallow them whole. You might see your child physically cringe, look embarrassed, or even respond with anger. What does it mean, and how can you handle it? Should you stop praising your child?

The best thing you can do as a parent is to understand the situation a bit better. Below are a few reasons why some children are very uncomfortable with praise and what you can do about it.

Your child feels pressured to perform

Children often feel pressured when they have to put in a lot of effort to achieve a goal. They may have had to get entirely out of their comfort zone. When giving high praise, they may feel that they did it this time but might not be able to do it again. When praised, the stress and pressure they feel compounds, so they act negatively or look upset.

Don't focus on the achievement but rather the effort and hard work your child put in. Instead of saying, "Well done for winning the gold medal", you can say something like, "I noticed how hard you have been working on this project, and I must say I am very impressed."

Your child is self-conscious

Praise will draw attention to your child, who then feels self-conscious. Self-conscious children often feel anxious and judged by everyone else.

Self-conscious children are more receptive to one-on-one praise done in private. Write your praise on a card, whisper it in their ear, or pat them on the back with a thumbs-up instead of giving loud, verbal praise in public.

Your child has a negative self-image

When children have a negative self-image, it is often the reason for lashing out or acting angry and evasive when praised. If your child doesn't believe that he/she is brilliant or outstanding, the praise can merely shine a spotlight on how they feel and increase their negative feelings of self-judgement. They want the feelings to stop, so they lash out.

Try to tone down the praise slightly and be more descriptive than you would be with other children. For instance, instead of saying "Wow, you're amazing" or "You are brilliant and so talented", say something like "You really did a good job on your art project" or "I quite liked what you did with your new bedroom layout." Make it more of a statement paired with a sincere smile than enthusiastic praise.

Chapter Five: Approaching Discipline Calmly (without Anger, Ranting, or Frustration)

Disciplining children at home leads to happy, well-rounded adults. Unfortunately, discipline isn't always easy. Some days you want to scream, rant, and rave at your children. Don't worry; you're not alone. Millions of parents the world over have the very same feelings. What matters is how you deal with these feelings and how you react to your children at that moment.

Some days being a parent is downright challenging, and often the intricacies of disciplining your children can work on your last nerve. How do you avoid getting irked and discipline your children effectively when they are acting out? How do you discipline a naughty or outspoken child without getting angry, ranting or feeling overwhelmed with frustration? These are questions that this chapter will address.

First things first, don't fall into the trap of thinking that other parents have it all worked out. You are certainly not the only parent flailing around, unable to get it right. Many parents have the same struggle, and those who do have it right merely have a strategy.

Before we take a look at effective disciplining methods, let's first discuss how to handle your anger towards your children.

How to Manage The Anger You Have Towards Your Children

If your children have been pushing your buttons, you may feel tempted to act like a child yourself and have a tantrum. A vital thing to remember is that regardless of how your children behave, they are not your enemy. You may feel overwhelmed with anger, and that's when fight or flight mode sets in. Your body tenses, your mind races, your heartbeat quickens, and it feels impossible to stay calm.

Handling your anger is vitally important at this stage. You may feel as if you need to act immediately to teach your children a lesson, but if you do, you might end up spanking your children or yelling at them unnecessarily. You probably don't want to do anything that you will regret, and you may also want to use it as a teachable moment. What would the lesson be? By handling your anger and dealing with discipline and punishment calmly, you will be teaching your children that shouting, yelling, ranting, and getting out of control are not the go-to ways to solve problems. You will also be teaching them that they should not accept those are behaviours from other people when they are older (that refers to friends, colleagues, and life partners). Essentially, managing your anger towards your children could set the scene for a brighter and happier future in their relationships to come. In this way, children learn how others should treat them. If you want to manage the anger you have towards your children; you need to commit to the following:

- No hitting or spanking

- No swearing

- No name-calling

- No ridiculing

- No accusations

- No emotional blackmail

- No dishing out of punishment while angry

- No screaming, yelling, or ranting

Tips for Calm Disciplining

Being cool, calm, and collected is the first prize when it comes to discipline. The objective should be to teach your children that part of being mature and growing up is managing anger and taking responsibility for our actions. Below are a few tips to get the message across calmly.

Set limits before you lose your temper

When you get angry and feel out of control, it's usually because your children are doing things that push your buttons. In most instances, they do it because you haven't set boundaries and clear limits. The moment you feel yourself getting angry because your children behave unacceptably, intervene and redirect the behaviour. Do this before there's time for your frustration levels to rise. Ensure that your children know what you expect of them and what they can expect from you if they push the limits. Let your children know when your anger levels are rising. For instance, you can let the kids know that their squabbling gives you a headache and ask them to stop. If you have to ask again, let them know that a third strike means punishment (state what that punishment will be).

Only take action when you are calm

Disciplining your children will rarely be an emergency. Remember that it can wait. When worked up, take a few deep breaths. Walk away. Mention that you will discuss the matter later and take some time out to calm down. Go and do something to relieve the tension. Scroll through funny memes on your mobile phone, watch amusing videos on YouTube, go for a run or do something that gets you to a calmer place as quickly as possible. Once you are there, you can think about how to handle the situation.

Remember, you don't *have* to act on your anger

Anger can be a rather "loud" emotion. It can almost feel as if it is telling us to take action. Anger can spur you on to do and say things that you wouldn't usually, so it stands to reason that an angry reaction is not always the most reasonable. It's a good idea to listen to what your anger is telling you. Try to determine why you are outraged, what the angry voice is telling you to do (yell, shout, throw things) and then figure out if there's a way you can ensure you feel and act differently the next time a challenging situation arises.

How to Discipline Effectively

Disciplining children is a fine art. Forethought and care are paramount in disciplining. Shouting at your children and applying rash punishments won't lead to happy, well-balanced children. Discipline is not a punishment. It's a way of teaching children an alternative way of being.

The word discipline comes from the Latin word "disciplinare", which translates to "to teach" in English.

To serve a purpose, children must understand why what they are doing is wrong and what the correct behaviour should be. They should also understand the meaning behind the punishment. Children should never feel like the enemy, that you are picking on them or just trying to be mean when you punish them. Instead, they should accept that the punishment fits the "crime" and that being accountable and responsible is a part of maturing and growing up.

Consider the following when disciplining your children:

Make positive reinforcement a priority

Many parents believe that discipline is sudden and involves a punishment to correct behaviour. Instead, discipline should be continuous in the form of positive reinforcement. Think of it as a form of maintenance of your children. Just like it's better to regularly maintain your car to ensure its good health and longevity, disciplining your children is just as important. Effective positive reinforcement is about being specific, selective, positive, and encouraging. Don't praise your children only when they report that they have done something right. Look out for opportunities to catch them in the act of being good or even being kind, and then praise them specifically, by name, for the action. This type of reinforcement makes them want to do more of what gets them positive attention and less of what gets them negative attention.

Scrap the words "don't" and "no" from your discipline vocabulary

If all you ever do is shout "don't do that!" and "no!" your children will understand that you don't like what they are doing, but they won't know why or what an alternative behaviour should be. Instead of saying, "I said you *don't* run in the house!" say, "Remember to walk because you won't slip on the tile floor then." Practice rephrasing how you instruct and verbally discipline your children.

Suggest a do-over opportunity

If your children rush into the room and interrupt conversations, are rude to a guest, and make a racket, do you yell and send them out, or is there a better way to handle the situation? Everyone deserves a second chance to do things the right way. Instead, ask the children calmly to quieten down and point out kindly, but firmly, what they have done wrong. You could say, "You are making a lot of noise, and you almost knocked Aunty Sue right off her feet. Can you leave the room and then come back and try that again?" You may need to prompt your child to apologise to Aunt Sue, but treat it as a learning process and not as a punishment. Don't worry; your guests will respond well to the positive way you handle the situation.

Decide and agree on the consequences ahead of time

Remember that your children are part of your family "community". To participate in it, they must understand all of the community rules and regulations, just like we all have to listen to the government and abide by the country's laws. If we break the law, there is a predetermined punishment or consequence to face. Having an understanding of those laws is what keeps many people behaving like law-abiding citizens.

It works much the same in a family unit. Sit down with the family and discuss unacceptable behaviours. Attach inevitable consequences to certain "crimes" – make a note of these in a journal or notebook. Refer to it when the children misbehave or push your buttons. If they know what the rules are, they must face the consequences of breaking them. This understanding will create a level of respect between you and your children and teach them to be accountable for their actions. Being accountable will also encourage them to be mature about rules and laws when they grow older. People who know what the rules are in life are happier in general.

Chapter Six: Creating Family Rituals

When on a mission to raise happy, confident and well-rounded children, family rituals play a rather large role. Family rituals can have far-reaching effects on the life of a child. Children exposed to and participating in family rituals have:

- Increased happiness

- Emotional well-being

- A sense of belonging

- A strong sense of identity

- Confidence in group environments

- Success in school

- A sense of security

- Stronger family relationships

- Respect for family members

- Deep-rooted family values

All of the above contributes to children developing into happy, grounded, and confident adults. If you don't have family rituals in place already, now is a great time to start.

8 Family Rituals & What They Teach Children

You can incorporate several family rituals into daily life that will inspire positivity, responsibility, mutual respect, kindness, and compassion in children. Implementing some of these rituals will also help your children form stronger family bonds with you and their siblings. You should add to this list.

Family mealtimes

Pick a mealtime where the family will eat together. Most families choose to gather for the last meal of the day, but breakfast can also work quite well. The family should gather together, share a meal, share news from the day, and then help each other wash the dishes. It's a team effort, so think of it as family team building. Spending time together and sharing news helps you and your children to get to know each other better. Knowing what is going on in each other's lives is the best way to create strong family bonds.

Special dinner night

This family ritual expands on the above point. You can capitalise on each family member looking forward to a favourite meal. Pick one night a week or one night a month where you will cook a favourite meal. Have a roster so that the family knows when their favourite meal night is coming up. It makes each member of the family feel valued and unique.

Have a weekend family day at least once a month

Choose one weekend night or day each month where the family gets together for something fun. It can be a game of catchers in the garden, a snowball fight in the winter, playing board games, eating dinner at a restaurant, or movies and pizza night by the fireplace. It can even be a day set aside for a family project, such as sprucing up an old item of furniture or painting and decorating a family member's bedroom. Again, think of this as teambuilding.

Nurture giving activities

Families that volunteer together will grow closer while learning to be kind, compassionate, and giving to others. Set a day every few months where the whole family shares their time volunteering at an animal shelter or soup kitchen. You could also work together to collect food for the homeless or raise money for a charity as a family. These activities are an excellent way for children to work together to benefit other people (or animals).

Bedtime rituals

When your children go to bed at the end of the day, it shouldn't be an abrupt and disconnected event. Make it special. Make it a tradition to do certain things before bedtime. For instance, if your children go to bed at 8 pm, perhaps implement a 7.30 pm cup of tea. Sit together and enjoy your tea before heading to the bathroom with your children to oversee teeth-brushing. Then tuck them into bed and read them a bedtime story. Suppose you have older children that don't want to be tucked in or read bedtime stories, encourage some quiet time in bed, reading to themselves before going to sleep. Say goodnight every night, even if you are away (you can phone in to say goodnight). It reiterates to your children just how much you value them.

Have anything-goes birthdays

Making children feel special on their birthdays is a great way to make them feel a sense of belonging. Implement birthday traditions that they will remember even as adults, such as allowing your children to eat anything they want for breakfast on their birthday. Make sure that they pick their meals in advance to make them easier to arrange. Accept it and celebrate along with them. It's just one day, and it will make them happy for years to come.

Pet care

If you have pets, make sure that you involve the children in the process of caring for them. Caring for pets is an ongoing family ritual that teaches love and compassion as well as responsibility. Task the children with feeding the pet, cleaning its bedding/cage, and helping with all pet-related things.

Adventures

Make going on adventures part of your family rituals. Children need to explore and discover things, not just alone, but with their family members too. Going on adventures is a great way to nurture strong family bonds and create fun memories simultaneously. Of course, there isn't always time for outings and adventures, so try to make it a quarterly thing. Plan a big adventure every few months. You can find hikes to go on, museums to visit, fun parks to attend. Or you can create adventure treasure hunts that take you and the children through new areas. Alternatively, be tourists for a while. You can research places of interest and activities in your area and surrounds and plan to go on them.

Chapter Seven: Creating & Exploring Interests

Healthy, happy, and prosperous children have interests and passions. How can you help your children to develop interests and passions of their own? What if your children are resistant to the process? Many parents want the answers to these questions. The answer is simple; you have to *help* your child try out a few new things, and you have to be there throughout the entire process to provide support, encouragement, and even a shoulder to cry on (if the need arises).

By exploring your children's various interests, you can help them discover what their passions genuinely are. More than that, you can also help them to recognise what their strengths and weaknesses are. Taking healthy risks, exploring potential passions, and becoming more aware of strengths and weaknesses can provide an excellent self-esteem boost for children and teens.

Children with hobbies and pastimes can:

- De-stress and blow off steam

- Experience a sense of accomplishment

- Avoid boredom

- Build self-esteem

- Develop intrapersonal skills

- Share their talents with the world

- Develop relationships with peers (not in the same school as them)

Activities That Can Create Interests and Passions in Children

Let's look at several activities that you can try with your children to spark an interest in them. It's a good idea to try some of these activities more than once and in different settings. You might find that your children are more receptive to trying new things in private settings first, so be open to allowing them to find their feet and learn at their own pace.

Climbing, hiking, and biking

If you have energetic children, introduce them to climbing, hiking, and biking. All of these activities will appeal to the part of them that likes to be always on-the-go. They also get to experience a healthy activity that could turn into a lifelong passion. Climbing, hiking and biking are often enjoyed alone or as part of a team, so they are an option for introverted and extroverted children.

Art

Art isn't for everyone, but encouraging your children to join a class is an excellent idea if they show an interest in painting or drawing. Children can attend drawing, painting, sculpting, scrapbooking, pottery, and many other art classes. Art is a great way to develop motor skills and helps children express the unique way they see the world.

Learning a musical instrument

If you have children that love to sing and show an interest in music, expose them to the idea of learning how to play musical instruments. Playing a musical instrument is an excellent release for many people, and it's also a perfect way to keep your children occupied with something (and out of trouble). Ask your children if there's a specific instrument they would like to play. What's great about music is that it uses various parts of the brain simultaneously (it's excellent for brain development) to manage emotion, movement, and rhythm.

Collecting items

Some children develop an interest in collecting things. Collecting things is excellent for children who like to compare items, research things, and learn more about something. It's a great hobby for the enquiring and analytical mind. Children can be encouraged to collect stamps, shells, comic books, flowers (pressed), coins, rocks, CDs, vintage bottles, and similar. This type of hobby is usually carried well into adulthood.

Learning to garden

Many children get excited about gardening. They take an interest in seeing something growing and flourishing, and the fact that they have a hand in the process is very empowering. You don't have to set your children to work doing yard work daily, but rather encourage your children to set up a small hydroponic system to grow leafy greens or even do a bit of container gardening with flowers and veggies.

Cooking or baking

Not all children love to cook or bake as much as they love to eat the result. Some children want to be involved in the entire process of making baked goods or the meal. Your child might end up being an aspiring chef! Expose your children to cooking. Let them lend a hand at mealtimes and teach them how to make specific meals. There are cooking and baking classes available for children, so consider booking one too.

Chapter Eight: Teaching Children to Manage Emotions

Many parents are concerned about their responsibility when it comes to teaching children to manage their emotions. It's okay if you don't fully understand *why* you have to teach your children this or how to go about it. The good news is that it's never too late to start.

It's important to teach children to work through their emotions as it directly impacts their mental health. Children trained to express themselves will get into a routine of doing so. They will also learn healthy coping and response mechanisms to avoid negative coping patterns, resulting in depression, poor mental health, anxiety, and unhappiness.

When you teach your children to manage their emotions, they:

- Are more confident

- Become mentally strong

- Learn how to self-soothe

- Communicate clearly and effectively

- Have decreased anxiety

- Develop emotional intelligence

- Are less stressed

Teaching your children to manage their emotions equips them for all areas of life. They are sure to experience emotions in the classroom, on the playground, when socialising with friends, when co-existing with siblings, when reacting to you (the parent), and when getting into relationships with other people in the future.

How to Teach Children to Deal with their Emotions Healthily

Knowing that you need to teach your children about emotions and learning *how* to do that are two completely different things. Let's look at a few ways that you can try to teach your children what their emotions are and how to handle them better.

Set a good example

If you are the type of parent who rants and shouts whenever you are upset or angry, you are setting a bad example. Children need to see how you handle emotional situations so that they can model their behaviour on yours. You may not know it, but your children are watching everything you do, and they are learning from it. If you are calm when you get bad news, they will soon start to view that as the "right" way to be when they get bad news. If you scream and shout at your partner, your children will believe that it's acceptable to do that when upset with their family, friends, and partners in the future. Be careful about setting a bad example. The work begins with *you* first.

Encourage children to take time out when they feel mad/angry

Children will get angry with each other and with you. Calmly teach them that when they feel angry and want to scream, shout, throw things or say nasty things, they should excuse themselves and go for a walk to calm down. You can catch your children in a rage and calmly request that they practice the coping technique you taught. The more you encourage and remind your children of this method, the more they will become comfortable doing it. They will remember this as they grow older and face frustrating situations.

Teach children to name feelings

Teaching children to name feelings is an excellent way to help them recognise what other people might be feeling. Naming feelings also allows children to understand their feelings better. You can start teaching children essential emotion words from a young age, such as angry, sad, happy, and nervous. As your children grow older, you can focus on books and television programs. Stop and point to a character in a picture book and ask your children how they feel. You can do the same in a television program.

Talk about feelings regularly

Not a lot of people realise how important it is to ask their children how they are feeling. Try to ask your children every day to share with you how they are feeling. It would help if you also used the right language to help your child understand how feelings can impact situations. For instance, you can say, "I am sad that you didn't want to share your toys with Sophie at school" or, "You look thrilled playing with that doll. What do you like most about your doll?"

Reflect back

Telling children that they shouldn't feel a certain way is counterproductive. Often, we can't help how we feel regardless of how old we are. Ensure that your children know that they can share their feelings with you, even if it's not a nice feeling. Reflecting their feelings to them in an accepting and caring way can make them feel heard and rethink how they feel and why. For instance, instead of saying, "Don't throw your brother's toys out the window!" you can say, "It looks like you are angry with your brother. Can you tell me how you feel while we go and fetch those toys?" Look for ways to deal with the feelings constructively.

Create safe and healthy outlets for venting

Just like adults, sometimes children need to vent. As a parent, you don't want to force your child to stifle emotions. You want to give them the freedom to be able to express their feelings. Sometimes, children's emotions are complicated, and they need to vent safely and healthily. Teaching your children how to vent instead of yelling, shouting, and throwing things is an excellent way to ensure that they lead healthier and happier lives in adulthood. The outlets your children are given will be things that they can turn to throughout their lives. Some safe ways for children to vent are punching a punching bag (you may want to invest in one for the children) and listening to loud music (get your child some earphones for this one). Some children don't want to get physical to vent or let off steam. If your children are like this, you may want to encourage having a bubble bath, ordering their favourite junk food, going for a walk or run, or getting lost in a good book/magazine.

Chapter Nine: Helping Children Build Meaningful Relationships

As your children grow and develop, you will no longer be their only focus point. They will begin to seek the company and attention of other people. Of course, you want your children to grow into adults who have good friends and a sturdy support system. Having good friends can only happen if your children learn how to build meaningful relationships from a young age. Children can benefit in the following ways from relationships:

- They know how to think for themselves

- They develop an understanding of other people

- They develop better communication skills

- They learn to express their emotions better

- They develop social skills

As your children develop into adults, they will also understand how networking works, which will help them in school and a career.

4 Ways to Help Your Children Make Friends & Develop Relationships

There several ways that you can help your children to have satisfying relationships with other people. You have to be willing to help your children to step out of their comfort zone. It can be challenging for a parent. It's difficult to see your child struggling to communicate with other children, and it's tough to let your young child sleepover at a friend's house. It's hard because your priority is to protect your child, but keeping your child at home and away from others will only result in them being lonely and unfulfilled later on in life.

Below are a few ways to ensure your child's immediate and future happiness by helping him/her make friends and build good relationships.

Be interested

Before your children start trying to form relationships with other people, they have to be of the mindset that they are interesting, wanted, and worthy. Children can only develop those feelings if they are shown and taught them. By being interested in your children and their activities, you show them that they are valued and worthy of having friends. Feeling worthy is an essential foundation for making friends. Confidence will go a long way.

Create opportunities for your child to make age-appropriate friends

There will be several opportunities for you to introduce your children to other children of the same age. Perhaps you can arrange playdates with other mums from the same playschool, or you can enrol in a kids and parents club. Socialising with other children is important because children need to learn and consistently practice being a friend. It doesn't always come naturally. For instance, your children need to learn to share their toys, take turns, solve conflict calmly, have fun, and understand how their behaviour makes other children feel.

Spending time at a play centre can be used as an opportunity to teach your children to develop meaningful relationships. You can first encourage your children to help other children who might be struggling to reach a toy, get something to work or get onto playground equipment. You can also make a point of gently asking your children how their behaviour could have impacted another child. For instance, you might say, "I noticed you wouldn't let Sam play with any of the toys. Do you think that could have hurt Sam's feelings?"

Teach your children the art of conversation and sharing

Good friends are the ones who share their news with you and know how to chat. Not many children have this skill; they are often dumped in front of the TV and expected to be quiet when adults are talking. Below are a few ways you can help your children become better conversationalists at any age include:

- Talk to your children often and be conversational. Making conversation exposes them to the concept of chatting and sharing, and they will start to see it as usual.

- Read a few books on hobbies and news that would interest your child. You can use this knowledge to engage with your child in a conversation about these topics.

- Ask your children questions when they are telling you something. Asking questions will teach them to be more descriptive and how to entertain while telling a story. A great way to practice this with your children is to play the Chit-Chat game. To play this game:

1. Write down a few possible topics on a piece of paper and put them in a jar.
2. At breakfast or evening mealtime, pull out a topic and get the children talking and discussing that topic.
3. Ask as many questions as possible. You may start to notice that your children have opinions!

These are just a few of the ways that you can teach your children to converse better.

Host sleepovers

You can encourage your children to make friends with the right people by guiding them through their first sleepovers. If you have friends with children of a similar age, invite them to a sleepover for a weekend. Start with one friend at a time at first. For children, being friends is about having something unique. It's a strong bond. Make the sleepover special for them. Let them play games they like, provide them with their favourite snacks and make the whole occasion fun. Provide the perfect opportunity for them to create happy memories with each other. If you notice that it works and your children are connecting with others, encourage them to keep the friendship up by having follow-up play dates, sending a fun card on a birthday, arranging fun outings together and so on.

Chapter Ten: Implementing a Healthy Daily Schedule

When your children grow up into independent adults, you want peace of mind that you did everything possible to teach them how to look after themselves and lead a healthy lifestyle. A healthy lifestyle takes care of physical, mental, and emotional wellbeing. If your child knows how to take care of those three areas, they will lead longer and healthier lives. You can also feel good that they will go on to teach their children the same healthy-living sentiments.

Happy and prosperous children are physically, mentally, and emotionally healthy.

7 Ways to Create a Healthy Lifestyle for Your Children

Implementing a healthy daily schedule is a great way to get your children on the right track. How do you go about creating a healthy plan for your children? Below are a few pointers.

Lead by example

If you're living on pizzas and chips and neglecting to exercise and take time out to relax, you're setting a poor example for your children. Again, the work needs to begin with you. You have to lead by example. Show your children that you are making healthy food choices. Serve healthy balanced meals during the week and allow some junk food and snacks on the weekends. Children will have something to look forward to and make healthier choices most days of the week.

Establish a regular sleep schedule

Kids and teens will fight against sleep time, but don't budge on it. Bedtime is bedtime – no negotiations! If your children claim that they aren't tired, allow some reading time in bed or some quiet time in their rooms before sleep. It doesn't matter what ages your children are; having a set time to go to bed and wake up every day is the only way to ensure that your children develop a healthy sleeping pattern and truly get enough sleep hours.

Make daily exercise compulsory

It's a sad reality that thousands of children suffer from obesity and unnecessary health issues because they never exercise or don't do enough exercise. All children should do at least 30 minutes minimum of exercise per day. High-intensity exercise is always best. If you don't want to send your children to the gym, think about creating a home exercise area. You can buy gym equipment, but you don't need to. You can buy a few dumbbells, yoga mats, exercise balls and then write down a list of exercises and how many times they should do them.

Make sure that completing the activities forms part of your children's daily schedule. Other options include going for daily walks, walking the dog, or joining after-school sports. Exercise is good for burning off energy but also helps with weight control and healthy bodily functions. Your children will thank you later on in life when they look forward to exercising, and it has become a habit.

Encourage children to drink plenty of water

Water is not the first choice for many children. Society has done a fine job of pushing sugar on children, so their go-to drinks usually end up being soda or fruit juice (full of sugar). Encourage your children to have at least four glasses of water each day. You can serve a glass of water with each meal and encourage them to sip on water between meals. Teach children that water is essential to healthy bodily functions, and for teens, it can do wonders for spotty skin.

Get your children out into the sunlight

Much the same as exercise, children need at least 30 minutes of sunlight each day. If you're unable to ensure that amount for your children, you should consider a vitamin D supplement. Vitamin D, free from the sun, is essential for healthy bones, teeth, and mental health. Researchers have found that vitamin D plays a role in regulating moods, so it should come as no surprise that you and the children generally feel happier after spending a day in the sun. Start by getting the children to go for walks, play outside, or sit in a sunbeam when available.

Draw up weekly schedules for the children

A whiteboard can help draw up a weekly schedule. Draw up the days of the week and make sure that you assign healthy tasks for each day. You can also note what activities each child is doing each day, including exercise (or sports), chores, and meal plans. A visual representation ensures that family members are more likely to stick to it.

Set screen time limits

Children nowadays spend their time glued to screens. Too much screen time essentially makes them miss out on life and genuine connections. It's a good idea to help your child to understand healthy screen time limits. For instance, your children should not be on their mobile phones for at least one hour before bed. You can set a certain amount of television hours that each child can watch each week. Log the hours in a notebook if it helps. For instance, your oldest child can get 3 hours of TV per week. She can choose how and when to spend those hours (within reason) but once used; she must find alternative ways to spend her free time.

Don't just limit screen time, but also suggest healthy alternative activities, such as playing a board game, listening to music, getting stuck into a good book, painting or drawing, chatting with the family, or delving into a hobby (crocheting, scrapbooking, writing, photography and so on).

Chapter Eleven: Teaching Action and Consequence

You might be wondering why you need to teach your children about action and consequence if you want to help them grow into well-rounded, responsible and happy adults. The reality is that children need boundaries to grow and flourish. Boundaries come in the form of predictable expectations and consequences.

Understanding the consequences helps children:

- Feel safe and secure

- Develop a less oppositional attitude

- Understand the rules of engagement with others and the rest of the world

- Misbehave less

- Understand what is expected of them

- Understand what the punishment is if they misbehave, break a rule, or do something unacceptable

- Adopt a positive outlook on life

When you teach children about consequences, you tell them that they matter and what they do matters too. Children need to come to an understanding that the decisions they make and the actions they choose to take have an effect on others and the world. The consequences of decisions and actions can be both positive and negative.

To effectively teach your children how essential consequences are; you have to do three things:

- Set realistic expectations

- Act consistently (you should never withhold consequences)

- Help your children reflect on their choices and actions (both good and bad)

Help Your Children Grow and Learn Through Their Choices and Decisions

By making your children accountable for their actions and decisions, you can help them grow and learn. Below are several ways that you can help your children to be more responsible. Responsible children are happy children.

Avoid threats but set expectations

Before entering any situation with your children, talk gently to them about expectations of their behaviour. For instance, if you visit a book store or library, you can chat with your child about the importance of being quiet. Mention that you will have to leave and go straight home if he/she cannot play by the rules. Make sure that your child knows that book stores and libraries have a "be quiet" rule. Also, be optimistic about it. Let your child know that you believe he/she can be great in the book store or library. Doing this sets a clear expectation, and there is also a specific consequence if they don't meet that expectation.

Discuss natural consequences with your children

Children shouldn't blindly follow the rules without understanding why. They also shouldn't blindly accept the consequences without understanding why. Take some time to discuss natural consequences with your children.

First, grab a piece of paper and create a list of unacceptable behaviours and broken rules with the consequence written next to them. For instance, if your child doesn't take out the trash on his turn, he will have to help his siblings take out the garbage on their days for the rest of the week. Now, ask your children to consider why that consequence is in place and what the natural consequences might be. For instance, when your child decides not to take the trash out, someone else has to do it, which is unfair (this is a natural consequence). Also, trash left inside can overflow and be unhygienic to the entire family, which is another natural consequence.

Another example is not brushing teeth. The natural consequence is bad breath and cavities leading to dentist visits. To get your children thinking of the real-world value of consequences, discuss many examples.

Use appropriate consequences for the "crime"

Many parents go about setting consequences wrongly because they believe that a consequence should be a punishment. Instead, try to use consequences as a way to teach children to act differently. It should be a learning moment, not a painful moment. For instance, saying that your child can't watch television with the family because she made a mess in her bedroom and hasn't cleaned it up is not the correct way to apply a consequence. A practical consequence for making a mess would be to instruct your child to clean it up and write an "I'm sorry" note about the mess. This consequence helps your children understand what they did wrong and provides them with the correct way to behave in future.

Be consistent with applying consequences

If you let your children off the hook a few times, they will stop taking consequences seriously and will start to believe that they can wangle their way out of them. Once you have set realistic expectations and consequences in place with your children, you need to act every time they misbehave, break a rule, or do something wrong. By being consistent, you are preparing your children for the real world. When they do something wrong in the real world (when they are older), the law (and other people) won't go easy on them.

Ensure that your children know to expect and count on consequences for each of their actions and decisions. You can also create a few good consequences in your home. For instance, if your children do a great job of cleaning up the house before you get home from work, you can spoil them to a double scoop of ice-cream for dessert. Positive reinforcement is valuable when it comes to consequences.

Use a reward system

You can also teach the value of consequences by using a reward system. Reward systems are ideal for parents who want to focus on an upbeat parenting style by reinforcing good behaviour. For small children, you can use a chart with stickers to motivate good behaviour. You can reward school-going children for good behaviour with outings and experiences (going to the park, visiting the animal shelter, for instance). You can focus on rewarding teens with pocket money and privileges in the home.

Chapter Twelve: The Importance of Prioritising Your Marriage or Relationship

All parents need to understand that their relationships are the first examples that their children have of relationships. They will view these relationships and consider them the norm.

If you and your partner portray a unified front and let the children see how much you value and respect each other, it provides them with a sound basis for their future relationships. You undoubtedly want your children to end up in loving, caring, and satisfying relationships. For this to be possible, you need to nurture your relationship to provide an example to your children. Whether you are married or have a steady partner, you need to prioritise it and let your children see just how joyful, valuable, and full of love it is.

Exposing your children to a bad relationship that is loveless, abusive, disrespectful, or unbalanced will be setting a low standard for your children to use when seeking out relationships of their own.

Prioritising your relationship ensures that your children:

- Feel safe and secure in the family

- Have a solid foundation to rely on

- Understand what a real loving relationship looks like

- Have a sense of how partners should treat each other

How to Set a Good Relationship Example for Your Children

To set a good example for your children when it comes to marriage and relationships, you need to prioritise your connection with your other half. Prioritising your partner doesn't mean that you put you and your partner first and your children second. It merely means that you do good things for your relationship and its future daily and let your children see it in action. Below are a few ways that you can do this.

Be affectionate

Your children need to see you and your partner being affectionate with each other. Of course, you should never go overboard, but make sure they see you hug and kiss each other when heading in separate directions for the day. Smile at each other. Be genuinely happy to see each other.

Go on dates

Your children might whine about you going out and having fun without them but do it anyway. Showing them that your partner is your favourite person and wanting to spend alone time together is essential.

Handle arguments calmly and with respect

Some parents have a rule of never arguing in front of the children, and while that can have value, it's not always possible. Sometimes it's perfectly fine to have a discussion instead of letting the tension build up until you are alone. Children can pick up on underlying tension anyway. If an unchecked argument crops up, speak to your partner respectfully, try to accept your part to play in the problem, and don't withhold affection or raise your voice. It may sound like a tall order, but it becomes second nature with a bit of practice. After all, this is how you should aim to treat someone you love.

Say "I love you" in front of the children

Children often look to their parents for security. If they suspect their parents aren't happy or are breaking up, it can cause an immense amount of stress for them. In a happy marriage or relationship, saying "I love you" should come easily. Don't be shy to say it in front of the kids even if they object and shriek, "Yuck!!" It's an essential thing for them to witness, for their future relationships.

Go to bed at the same time

It's sometimes difficult for parents to find time to spend alone together. Bedtime is a great time to do that, even if it's just to cuddle or read books in companionable silence. When you go to bed at the same time, and the kids see it, it reiterates that you are a unit and that you want to be together.

When talking to your partner, put your mobile phone away

Putting your mobile phone away when you spend time with your partner speaks a language your children will understand. Children spend loads of time glued to their screens, and they know that to get them to look up and pay attention, something significant needs to be happening.

When spending time chatting with your partner, make sure to put your mobile phone in your pocket or screen-down on the counter. Give your partner your undivided attention. Even if the children try to interrupt, make your partner's conversation a priority. Genuinely engage with your partner and respond. Make sure that the children see how meaningful and profound a relationship and special connection can be.

In Summary (Conclusion)

As a parent focusing on raising happy children in a patient and wholesome way, reading this book has been a step in the right direction. Put the tips and advice to use and you will feel proud as you watch as your children steadily grow and prosper into mature, happy adults. It's essential to focus on steady, long-term growth with your children. Don't try to rush it or force it. Instead, have a holistic approach to transforming your relationship with your children. Guiding your children to become healthier and happier is a work in progress. Always view it this way, and you won't succumb to stress and anxiety. Raising happy children is an ongoing task that requires consistent work. With the advice of this book, you are off to a good start. Remember that you are only human, and just by making positive changes, your children will notice that you are taking steps towards bettering their lives and yours - rest easy in that knowledge.

Before you put this book down, let's do a quick recap of what you have learned. Below is a summary (overview) of each of the 12 chapters in this book. Scan them periodically as a brief reminder.

Chapter One – Prioritising self-care

Prioritising self-care ensures that you are at your best for your children. It's also important to teach children to practice self-care by teaching children to:

- Be independent

- Make their own fun

- Care for their physical needs

- Self-soothe

Chapter Two – Creating an element of positive thinking

Children with a positive outlook are typically more successful at school and sport, less prone to mental health issues, more satisfied in relationships, less prone to depression and generally healthier. How to teach children to be more positive:

- Make positive notes

- Create "life's good" journals with your children

- Share fun and positive stories with your children

- Encourage children to carry out acts of service

- Expose children to fun and positive books

Chapter Three – Implementing family responsibilities (chores)

Children need to be part of the family "community" to develop a sense of belonging and understand that they play an integral role in the family unit. Things to remember when setting chores/responsibilities for children:

- Set clear expectations

- Get stuck in and help out

- Praise – give positive feedback

- Empathise and be persuasive

Chapter Four – Praising correctly

Praising children keeps them engaged, builds confidence, teaches self-pride and helps children to view themselves more positively. How to use praise the right way:

- Be specific about what you are praising

- Always praise when your children try something new

- Avoid praising too often or for *everything*

- Only praise genuinely and honestly

- Praise the effort put in and not the achievement/award

- Avoid using conditional praise

- Avoid using comparison praise

Chapter Five – Approaching discipline calmly

It's important to discipline children without anger, ranting, and frustration. Children need discipline. Children thrive when disciplined correctly. How to discipline calmly:

- Set limits before you lose your temper

- Only take action when you are calm.

- Remember, you don't *have* to act on your anger.

- Make positive reinforcement a priority.

- Scrap the words "don't" and "no" from your discipline vocabulary

- Suggest a do-over opportunity.

- Decide and agree on the consequences ahead of time.

Chapter Six – Creating family rituals

Children who participate in family rituals have increased happiness, better emotional well-being, a sense of belonging, healthy family relationships, and a sense of security. Consider encouraging children to participate in the following family rituals.

- Family mealtimes

- Special dinner night

- Have a weekend family day at least once a month

- Nurture giving activities

- Bedtime rituals

- Have anything-goes birthdays

- Pet care

- Going on family adventures

Chapter Seven – Creating and exploring interests

Children can become more aware of and comfortable with their strengths and weaknesses by exploring different interests. Expose your children to hobbies and activities, so they can decide what their passions are. Some activities to expose your children to include:

- Climbing, hiking, and biking

- Art

- Learning a musical instrument

- Collecting items

- Learning to garden

- Cooking or baking

Chapter Eight – Teaching children to manage emotions

When children are taught to manage their emotions, they are more confident, become mentally stronger, know how to self-soothe, can communicate clearly, have decreased anxiety, develop improved emotional intelligence, and are less stressed. You can teach children to deal with emotions in the following ways:

- Set a good example

- Encourage children to take time out when they feel mad/angry

- Teach children to name feelings

- Talk about feelings regularly

- Reflect back

- Create safe and healthy outlets for venting

Chapter Nine – Helping children build meaningful relationships

Children who know how to build and nurture positive and meaningful relationships stand to benefit in various ways. They will develop an understanding of other people, communicate better, learn to express their emotions, and develop appropriate social skills. You can help your children to form friendships and relations in the following ways:

- Be interested

- Create opportunities for your child to make age-appropriate friends

- Teach your children the art of conversation and sharing

- Host sleepovers

Chapter Ten – Importance of implementing a healthy daily schedule

Happy and prosperous children are physically, mentally, and emotionally healthy. Teaching your children to look after themselves and make healthy choices will stand them in good stead when they are adults. Seven ways you can help your children make healthier choices are as follows:

- Lead by example

- Establish a regular sleep schedule

- Make daily exercise compulsory

- Encourage children to drink plenty of water

- Get your children out into the sunlight

- Draw up weekly schedules for the children

- Set screen time limits

Chapter Eleven – Teaching children about consequences

Children who understand consequences are more prone to be law-abiding, fair, and responsible adults. When children are accountable for their actions, they feel more secure, develop a less oppositional attitude, behave better, know what is expected of them, and develop a positive outlook on life. You can help your children learn from their decisions and actions in the following ways:

- Avoid threats but set expectations

- Discuss natural consequences with your children

- Use appropriate consequences for the "crime"

- Be consistent with applying consequences

- Use a reward system

Chapter Twelve – Importance of prioritising your marriage/relationship

Setting a good relationship example for your children will help them to make good relationship choices in the future. Children who see parents prioritising their marriage or relationship feel more secure, have a solid foundation, understand what loving relationships look like, and have a better sense of how to treat a partner acceptably. Let your children witness you prioritising your relationship in the following ways:

- Be affectionate

- Go on dates

- Handle arguments calmly and with respect

- Say "I love you" in front of the children

- Go to bed at the same time

- When talking to your partner, put your mobile phone away

Congrats on taking this crucial step towards becoming the best parent you can be and helping your children develop into happy, well-rounded, and responsible humans.

Disclaimer

This book contains opinions and ideas of the author and is meant to teach the reader informative and helpful knowledge while due care should be taken by the user in the application of the information provided. The instructions and strategies are possibly not right for every reader and there is no guarantee that they work for everyone. Using this book and implementing the information/recipes therein contained is explicitly your own responsibility and risk. This work with all its contents, does not guarantee correctness, completion, quality or correctness of the provided information. Misinformation or misprints cannot be completely eliminated.

Printed in Great Britain
by Amazon

21140631R00064